Contents

Foreword: Your Mission

I suspect you don't want to just live your life.

Am I right? You want to love your life. You want to wake up in the morning inspired about the day ahead, knowing you're doing exactly what you're meant to do.

You want to feel your life has significance. And you want to deeply experience happiness, even when it arises in its simplest forms.

This book is your invitation to go beyond just living to thriving.

It's your guide to bursting out of standard conventions of how your life is 'supposed' to be and instead, treating your life as a canvas. Creating your own design. Envisioning and building a life that is completely your own beautiful, masterful work of art.

If you're like most people, you've been taught to chase goals. You've been told achievement is the yellow brick road to happiness.

You've been told wrong.

Achievement is marvelous. But there's a nasty, dark secret that lies beneath it: it will never lead to actual happiness unless it's tied to something bigger.

Fulfillment can only happen when you clearly understand who you are and align every career and life decision to what matters most to you, deep-down at the core of your being.

No matter what stage of life you're at right now, you can learn to thrive as a leader and in life.

So open your mind up to your wildest possibilities. And then, wider still.

Get ready to thrive.

Lisa Martin, PCC

Part One:

WHY ACHIEVING ISN'T THRIVING

A Story of Thriving

Let me tell you about my own journey with thriving. And not thriving.

A long time ago when I was an upstart PR maven, I consisted primarily of raw smarts and goals.

Oh how I loved a goal. Give me a mission and I would achieve it. I was unstoppable.

I encountered a particularly juicy goal in my late twenties. I'd heard about a small, niche PR agency that sold to a multinational for serious money and voila, my sights were set. I made it my mission to replicate this feat.

At the age of 28 I founded Cornerview Communications and faster than lightning I had a roster of clients that made the big guns in town take notice.

I gave myself 10 years to fulfill my dream to sell the business. I did it in less than three.

Suddenly I was 30, my wildest goal realized. And I felt something totally unexpected: dissatisfaction.

I thought reaching such an enormous goal would give me a few years (or at least several good months) of contentment. But no.

I can't describe my confusion. It was such a jarring disconnect with everything I believed about happiness.

Out of desperation, I began to investigate what it takes to thrive in life, not just achieve.

I threw myself into this new focus – reading, researching, attending conferences, interviewing experts. I was a woman obsessed.

I applied all this learning in my own life. My most fundamental change was this: Rather than chasing empty goals, I focused on aspirations that aligned directly to my personal values and vision of thriving.

It took less time than you might imagine to chart a new path for myself.

And guess what? I started to feel happy. Satisfied. I started enjoying the ordinary moments of my life rather than awaiting fleeting flashes of achievement. I became a better person.

I could see that I had tuned into something important. I could also see that there were legions of people struggling the way I had to find meaning in a goal-focused life.

I wanted to help people make the switch from living to thriving, and that's what I've been doing for the past 15 years as a leadership coach, speaker and author.

Thriving Is an Art Form

Now let's talk about what it takes to thrive.

Many people experience an ongoing sense of discomfort in life. It often appears as anxiety or stress. Or a nagging sense something isn't quite right.

These are signals your life is out of alignment.

This doesn't mean you're not amazing, productive or wildly accomplished. It means that the majority of your time is spent on tasks not aligned to what you most deeply want out of life.

You can never thrive if your life is misaligned. You will always feel slightly off. Less than deeply happy. Less than your true self. Less than.

People who thrive see their life as an art form, carefully aligning their everyday actions and decisions to a personal vision of thriving. Much like a painter styles a canvas to match a picture in the mind's eye.

People who thrive have a talent for living in alignment with their deepest desires. And they know thriving takes different shapes at various stages of life.

At one life stage, thriving could mean investing a huge percentage of your time and effort into your career because it engages and inspires you. Another stage could be about taking a sabbatical to pursue a crazy adventure. Yet another stage could be about finding harmony between parenting and career. Your life stages will be unique to you and your priorities.

Right now you might feel extremely close to fully thriving, but not quite. Or you may feel thriving is a distant, lofty dream.

Regardless of where you fall on the spectrum, you can learn this art form. Like any other creative pursuit, it will take self-awareness, knowledge and practice to master the art of thriving.

Your Life Is a Masterpiece

Beautiful lives are not manufactured by someone else. They're handcrafted by you.

To master the art of thriving, you'll need to put aside all thoughts of what you're 'supposed' to do and how you're 'supposed' to be. You'll need to resist convention and focus your life on your artistic vision.

In this sense, you need to become an artist to thrive. Your life is your expression and it will never be fully yours until you learn to live it on your own terms.

Just as Renoir, Monet and Gauguin were each entirely distinctive, you will need to create your own style. You will need to follow your own instincts. You will need to consciously choose the raw materials to use to create your life.

There is no single way to thrive. There are only your individual desires and your audacity to bring them to life.

To master the art of thriving, you'll need to:

1 Have a vision.

2 Assume anything is possible.

3 Make your own rules.

4 Resist convention.

5 Defer to your gut, not the opinions of others.

Before You Can Thrive

This book is a master's class that follows my previous guide, *Lead + Live: 6 Practices to Live Bigger,* where I present the foundational steps required for thriving.

I make reference in this book to concepts (like 'values' and 'purpose') that are discussed in detail in the previous book.

Without the Live Bigger Practices under your belt, the practices here can't take full effect for you. It would be like attempting to draw a fine self-portrait without first knowing how to sketch.

I encourage you to read the first *Lead + Live* if you haven't done so. It will prepare you for your journey to thriving.

Part Two:

MASTER THE ART OF THRIVING

The Method

Anyone can learn to thrive. You don't have to be a certain age, or at a particular point in your career.

This book is based on a self-coaching model that will help you develop greater self-awareness and understand the practices needed to thrive in your leadership and in life.

In this book you will find:

1 The **Thrive Model** that highlights the 6 practices you need to thrive.

2 An explanation of each **Thrive Practice** and why it matters.

3 **Four Advice Articles for each Thrive Practice** to deepen your understanding.

4 **One Leading Question for each Thrive Practice** to help you gain self-awareness.

5 **(Optional) Thrive Assessment.**

The Model

Let me introduce you to the **Thrive Model.**

HAPPINESS   VISION

WEALTH   MINDFULNESS

VOICE   VITALITY

This model is based on 15 years of leadership coaching in a vast cross-section of industries across North America.

In that time, I've delivered hundreds of workshops, coached thousands of people and conducted in-depth interviews with countless individuals who are thriving in all aspects of life.

This model is also deeply informed by my personal journey from discontented high-achiever to full-fledged thriver.

Through all of this, I've learned what distinguishes people who thrive from those who don't.

Without further ado, here are the 6 Practices to Master the Art of Thriving:

1 **Mindfulness:** Calm your mind and get focused.

2 **Vitality:** Live with enthusiasm and energy.

3 **Voice:** Speak with clarity and confidence.

4 **Wealth:** Get real about money.

5 **Happiness:** Believe in yourself and choose contentment.

6 **Vision:** Visualize your thriving life.

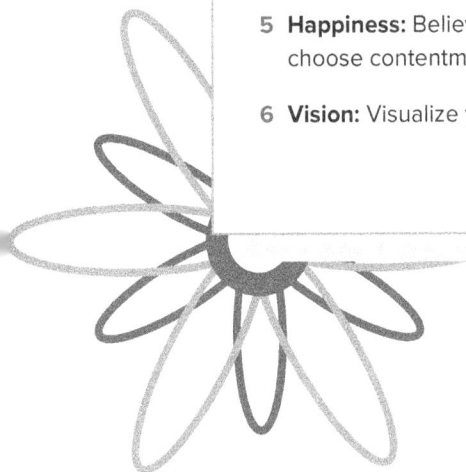

The 6 practices featured in this guide must be experienced as a set, which is to say, you can't select the ones that appeal the most and expect to fully thrive on your own terms.

All the practices require steady use. They are an integrated system, so it's essential to apply them all equally in your own unique way.

That's how you master the art of thriving.

Part Three:

THE 6 THRIVE PRACTICES

Mindfulness

It's impossible to thrive without being here, in the present moment, to really experience your life. This is **mindfulness**.

MINDFULNESS

The curious, troubling thing about work and life is you can get so caught up in chasing 'The Dream' that you entirely miss the amazing stuff that's actually happening, right now, in this very moment.

We're taught to seek and celebrate life's big occasions, but in reality your whole life is so much more constant and rich than that. You're literally missing your life if you're always looking to the future, waiting for your next big win.

People who thrive are those who can feel the beauty even in the smallest, seemingly insignificant moments. They know this is where joy lives.

People who aren't mindful tend to live in the past, reach for the future or coast on autopilot through life without ever soaking it in. Any of these options will cheat you out of the fullness of your life.

Being **mindful** may well be the simplest and most challenging thing you ever learn to do. At first, it may feel like you're slowing your life down. For busy, driven people, this can be frightening initially.

Then you realize you're not slowing it down.
You're taking it in.

Having a **mindful** dinner with your kids means your mind isn't drifting to work or home repairs or the fight you just had with your spouse. Your mind is focused on the taste of what you're eating, the words your kids are saying, the color of the sunset outside the kitchen window. It's focused on what's happening right now.

When you arrive at the office in the morning, rather than letting your mind toss and turn about a big presentation next week and a heated disagreement with a colleague yesterday, your mind clearly, calmly focuses on what needs to be done in this moment. Worrying won't make next week's presentation better and stewing won't repair yesterday's spat.

When you're in the moment, your mind opens up to far more possibilities. It can innovate. It can find solutions. It can operate with ease and efficiency. It can deeply hear and see what's going on around you, observing and learning at a much higher level. And most importantly, it can make clear, conscious choices at work and home. All of this means mindful people are steady, purposeful, compassionate and inspiring.

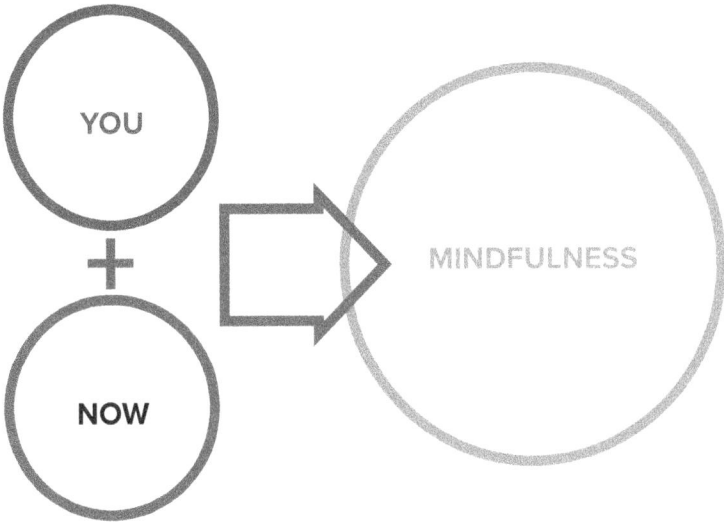

Mindfulness isn't like a light switch – it's not 'on' or 'off.' It's a continuum. No matter how mindful you are, you can always have more.

Are You Speeding Past Joy?

Oh there's so much talk about 'being in the present moment' and 'mindfulness,' but really what does it actually mean? Why does it really matter to people who are traveling at warp speed, with huge aspirations and weighty responsibilities?

It matters. Trust me.

Mindfulness isn't just a lot of new-agey banter. It is the very stuff of life.

You know those people who look back on their lives and ache with regret about the blurry memories of their kids' childhoods? They can recall a sizable list of achievements, but not the emotional highs that were supposed to accompany each one. They lacked mindfulness.

Soaking in the success of your life is about noticing the subtle moments of astounding joy that happen all the time ... if you allow them to. These moments need breathing room. They deserve airtime.

When I think of mindfulness, I like to recall my client Natalie who attended a mindfulness session with me a few years ago. She was a powerful, no frills kind-of-woman who previously believed mindfulness was a lot of hot air.

The weekend following my session, she found herself on an autumn stroll with her two adult daughters. They walked absentmindedly, chatting up a storm. Then – entirely out of character – Natalie said, "Let's stop. Look around ... drink this in."

And they stopped. And for a few moments they quietly absorbed the vibrant, multi-color spectacle that is fall in Ontario cottage country. The colors were deep and bold. The trees were enormous – awe-inspiring. All of it had been there all along of course, but none of them had noticed it until Natalie said, 'stop.'

That moment became a shared memory for Natalie and her daughters, and they still reminisce about the magic of that day. For Natalie, it was a turning point. She understood that there were moments like this in her life all the time. But she needed to allow herself to stop and experience them.

Don't Linger in the Past

I've seen some fabulously talented people kill their careers by lingering in the past. They didn't even know they were doing it.

Are you (unconsciously) clinging to some past glory or failure? If you are, it's keeping you from living up to your fullest potential today.

You need to be able to let go, acknowledging failures and successes, learning from them and moving on. I'm not talking about denying the past. I'm talking about not letting it hold you down.

Ask yourself these questions:

1 After an important conversation or meeting, do you spend a lot of time rehashing what was said and what you could have done differently?

2 Do you find yourself wishing you could go back in time and change something you did or said?

3 Do you hold a grudge?

4 Do you feel you missed an opportunity for happiness or success that you can never regain?

5 Do you feel you've passed your peak?

If you answered 'yes' to any of these questions, it's a warning bell that you might be lingering in the past. Start paying closer attention to how much importance and focus you place on past events.

When you catch yourself lost in the past, gently shift your focus to the present. Remind yourself the present is the only thing you can change. Remind yourself it's ok to let go.

A Busy Mind is Not Your Friend

We live in a world that loves busy people. Loves them.

It's a world that feeds us a steady diet of breaking news and mobile technology. We're told 'busy' means important. Successful. Fabulous. Normal.

But here is what's rarely mentioned: Busy minds aren't so wonderful when you're in a leadership role. And they don't allow space for happiness or thriving.

A stressed mind just breeds more stress. It's too preoccupied to see an easy path right in front of it and too busy to notice everyday moments of joy.

As a leader, you need to be clear-headed. You need to make sharp decisions. And, while this might be hard to hear, a busy mind is a scattered mind.

I see you shaking your fist at me. It sounds unfathomable to have a demanding career and active personal life without having a mind that's bursting at the seams.

I agree it's not easy. But I assure you, it's possible.

The Mindfulness Challenge

I challenge you to set a goal for yourself to have a calmer mind. I think you'll be surprised at how fast the benefits kick in.

Start by giving yourself 5 to 10 minutes in the morning (or at the end of the day) to put down all technology and just be still and silent. Just be.

Sounds painfully simple, right? Can you do it for 3 weeks straight?

It's likely you'll find your mind chattering non-stop at first, unable to take even a moment of true silence. That's ok. Go with it. When it chatters, talk back. Tell yourself, 'It's ok to be quiet for a moment. It's ok to not think right now.'

You also might find yourself drifting off, and then suddenly jolting alert again. That's ok too — it's not a problem.

Above all, be gentle with yourself as you experiment with mindfulness. Take great caution to not get frustrated or angry with yourself.

Your goal isn't a perfectly still mind. It's simply to play with letting it be calmer for a few minutes a day and accept whatever the experience brings.

How Mindful Are You at Work?

Let's speak candidly. You have priorities outside the office. Big priorities. And sometimes thoughts of those things seep into your consciousness as you're leading a meeting, giving a presentation or shaking hands with a new client.

You're human. It's all good. Don't beat yourself up about it.

Having said this, it's helpful to be able to wrangle the mind. And by wrangling, I mean gently, compassionately coaxing it to focus on the moment at hand.

Are you adept at this? How much time do you spend in the present moment, undistracted by other things?

Check out these 5 statements. How true is each for you?

1. When I'm working, I gently turn down thoughts of other things.

2. When someone at work speaks to me, I calmly focus on what they are saying. I don't plan my response as they speak.

3. I let problems at home leave my mind when I'm working.

4. I can sit in an hour-long meeting without checking the web or email.

5. I can focus on a task undistracted for an hour or two at a time.

If you confidently answered 'true' to 4 or 5 of these statements, you're often in the present moment as you're working.

If less than 4 of these statements are true for you, distraction is likely limiting your ability to focus. Trust me, you're not alone.

Take action now to improve your mindfulness. Pick 1 of the statements and commit to practicing it for the next 30 days. Don't worry about slip-ups along the way ... just keep going.

At first mindfulness comes in small, almost imperceptible steps. But even in its smallest doses, it's potent beyond belief.

Mindfulness

LEADING QUESTION

How much time do I spend with a calm, quiet mind?

Vitality

Vitality is a tangible exuberance for life that allows you to grow, change and thrive. It combines mental and physical vigor, making you a life force to be reckoned with.

HAPPINESS   VISION

WEALTH   MINDFULNESS

VOICE   VITALITY

Having **vitality** is possessing a huge capacity for life. It's being fully alive rather than going through life in partial measures. It's about having reserve energy that powers you through life's ups and downs.

Vitality allows you to take on new challenges: innovative projects, begin a new job, start a family ... really, any creative endeavor that requires a step up in your personal power.

People who have **vitality** in spades stand apart. They attack life with such gusto it's impossible to miss them.

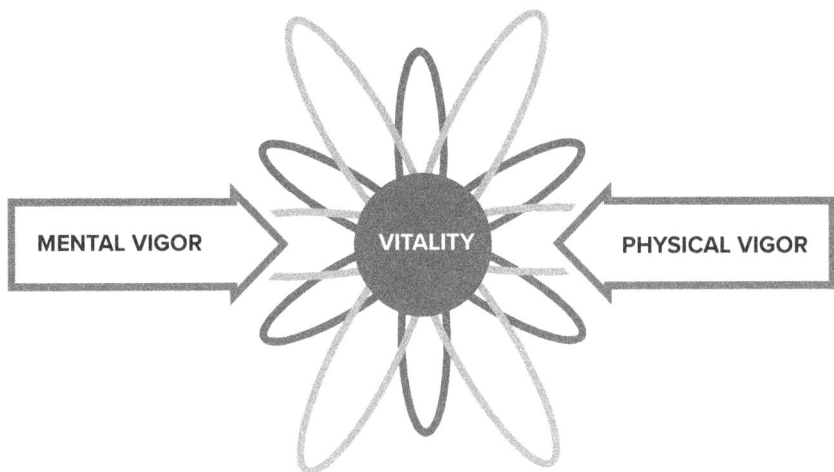

MENTAL VIGOR → VITALITY ← PHYSICAL VIGOR

In business and in life, this is an enormous asset. Vital people tend to naturally inspire and motivate others and because of this, they're more likely to land leadership roles. They also tend to recover from setbacks well and muster the energy needed to get the job done.

But here's a word to the wise: The more **vitality** you have, the more conscious you need to be of how those around you are reacting. **Vitality** can be intimidating and it can bring out other people's insecurities. That's no reason to limit your **vitality** or dim your brightness. It's simply a tip to make sure you're not steamrolling those around you.

Now, of course, everyone has hard days and difficult stretches in life. **Vitality** is not about denying reality and pushing yourself to be energized regardless of what's going on. It's important to let yourself feel the highs and lows of your life – including sorrow, anger, grief ... whatever may come.

But the question is, what is your typical **vitality** set point? In other words, all things being equal, are you generally a person with low, moderate or high **vitality**?

Vitality doesn't just happen – you need to fuel it. People get their energy from different sources, depending on their personalities.

To manage your **vitality** and fully thrive, you'll need to discover what gives you energy and what depletes you.

What's Your Vitality Level?

All things being equal, feeling vital should be your normal way of being. On an average, run-of-the-mill day, you should expect to feel energized about your life.

Does this surprise you?

Unless a recent event or situation is causing you to feel off -- like grief, sadness, anger or a random blue day — you have the right to feel pretty darn fantastic. If you don't, it's time to adjust your vitality level.

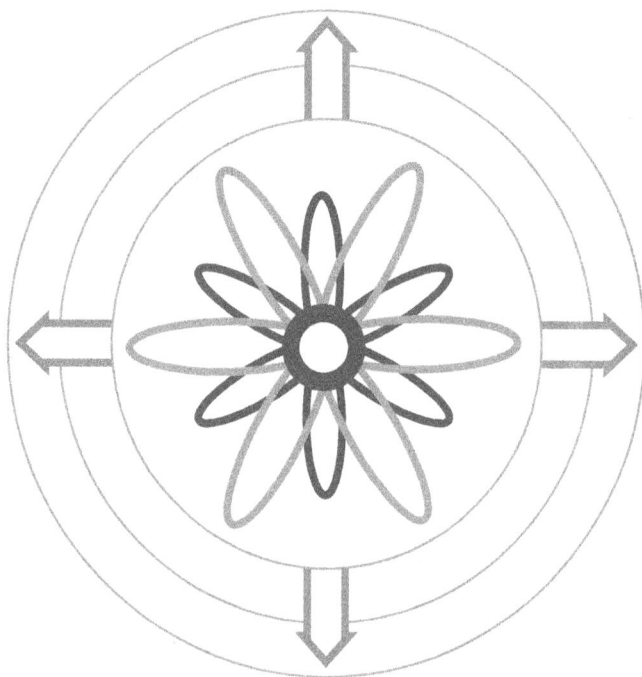

Here are 5 simple statements to help you determine if your vitality needs a boost. Be real with yourself ... how true is each one for you?

1 I wake up invigorated and ready to take on the day.

2 I can't wait to get to work in the morning.

3 I'm excited to hang out with family and friends.

4 I would describe myself as a joyful person.

5 I am often struck by how lucky I am.

Over the next several days, reflect on these statements and check your state of being. For example, when you wake up, notice ... are you feeling invigorated? How energized do you feel as you're heading into work or getting ready to spend time with family or friends?

If any of the 5 statements don't reflect your experience of life, take this seriously and kick-start a revitalization program. You deserve to regularly experience vitality. A lack of vitality will limit your ability to see your true potential and create the life you want.

If all of these statements are deeply true for you, congratulations on your high vitality level. Don't stop now. There's no cap on the amount of vitality you can have. A rigorous revitalization program will help you create even more.

What Energizes You?

Vitality doesn't just happen. It has specific, identifiable sources.

If you want to feel vital, you need to know your energy sources and feed your personal energy system. It's that straightforward.

What things in life give you energy? It's different for everyone. For some people, socializing gives them a tremendous boost. They leave a party feeling alive and bursting with vitality.

Others find it draining, even though they adore their family and friends.

Observe your patterns closely. I've found that many people are surprised by what they discover. Maybe they think watching TV (for example) is relaxing and restorative. But when they pay attention to how they feel afterward, they discover their energy is depleted.

This doesn't mean they should never watch TV. It just means they need to balance it with endeavors that will replenish their energy.

Make a list of things that boost your energy and keep it close by at all times. To get your ideas flowing, here are just a handful of common activities to consider. Do any of these feed your vitality?

What else is on your vitality list?

> Spending time in nature

> Exercising

> Listening to music

> Spending time with children

> Spending time with spouse/partner

> Socializing

> Going to church/spiritual activities

> Reading

> Cooking

> Artistic/creative projects

> Quiet time alone/self-reflection

> Learning new things

> Dancing

> Swimming

Start a Revitalization Program

Everyone needs time and space for revitalization and personal growth. This is common sense. It's how we maintain vitality … a zest for life.

So, why do so many people neglect to take the time?

Lack of capacity is the biggest reason. It stems from a belief that the world, as you know it, will end if you take time for rest and reflection. Projects will come to a screeching halt, colleagues will wander aimless and confused through your office corridors, family and friends will freak out en masse.

It's helpful to let go of the idea that giving yourself time to revitalize is somehow a disservice to society. This is a myth that has led many people to the dark, dismal corner of the universe known as burnout. Do not follow in their footsteps.

You're human. You need breathing room to pursue new thinking, process information and make needed changes in yourself. If it takes every ounce of your energy to just get through the day, you'll never find breathing room. You'll never evolve.

The biggest piece of advice I can offer is simply to schedule in rejuvenation time. I mean that literally. Pull up your calendar and schedule in time for workouts, walks in nature, journaling, spa days, weekend getaways, meditation, hiking … whatever restores you.

I have a client who scheduled monthly massages on her calendar and another who allotted weekly playground time with his son.

Inevitably, I see the same results again and again. When people make downtime a true priority, their stress level visibly drops. Their sense of ease comes back, along with their sense of humor.

Next thing you know, they're making decisions more swiftly. Tensions ease at home and work.

Treat your revitalization program with the same importance you give other commitments. If you don't take it seriously and you constantly postpone these vital activities, your capacity for life will suffer.

If your revitalization program is really humming, your capacity for life will expand. You'll be more clear-headed, productive and energized.

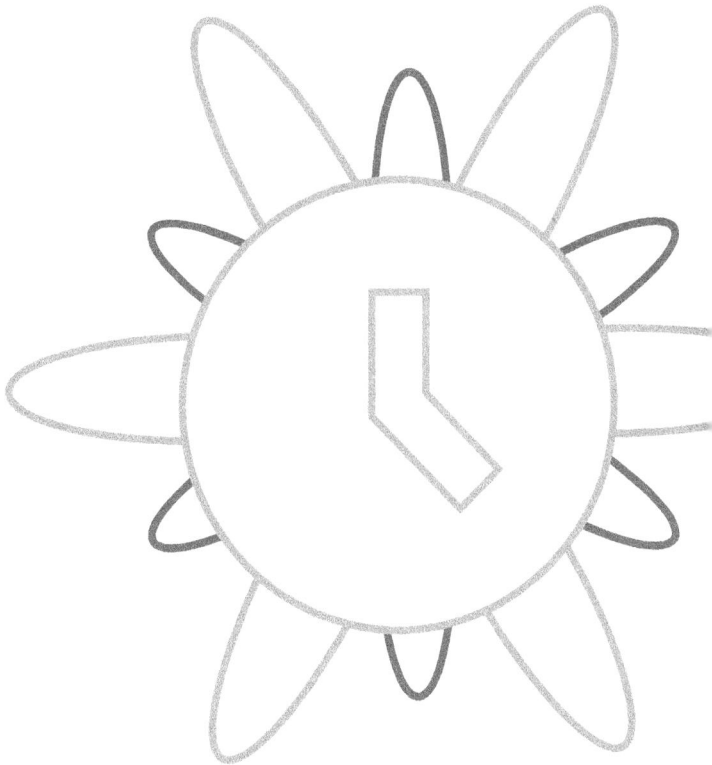

Know Your Vitality Leaks

Vitality leaks are probably sucking essential life-force energy from your body and mind. Right now.

Have you ever found yourself wanting to quit your job, not because you don't enjoy the work you do, but because the thought of your half-finished projects and impending deadlines is overwhelming?

A long list of unfinished tasks at home or work is a major vitality leak. As proof, just consider that lovely jolt of energy you get when you heroically cross a task of your list. That's you claiming some of your energy back.

Other common leaks are disorganization, clutter, regret, guilt, dissatisfaction and tough conversations you keep delaying.

You know when you open way too many programs on your computer and forget to close the ones you're not using anymore? Those unused programs are just there, sucking up your computer's resources, bogging it down. Your vitality leaks are doing this to your personal energy system.

If you want more vitality, take a hard look at what your stressors are and start eliminating as many as you can from your life.

Here's a 7-step process for fixing your vitality leaks:

1 Make an inventory of all the personal and work issues that are making you feel overwhelmed or stressed. Take as much time as you need to itemize them.

2 Look at each item and decide if you will start it, share it (delegate it to someone) or stuff it (let it go – move it off your radar once and for all). Note your decision beside each one.

3 Take your list of tasks to delegate ... delegate them immediately.

4 Next, choose 3 things from your 'start it' category. Assign dates to complete these 3 things.

5 Crucial step: live up to these completion dates. Check these 3 items off your list.

6 Celebrate. Seriously. Enjoy the energy that comes with completion.

7 Choose 3 more things from your 'start it' category and assign due dates. Complete them. Keep repeating this process.

You will likely never have a life absent of all vitality leaks, but that's not the point. The point is to manage and eliminate as many as possible.

Without question you'll notice a difference in your vitality level, allowing more energy to create and live the beautiful life you want.

Vitality

LEADING QUESTION

Am I willing to invest time to create more enthusiasm for my life?

Voice

This practice is about voicing your view. Using your **voice** is about being unafraid to vocalize what you really believe.

Using your **voice** effectively is a mark of a strong leader, wise parent and empathetic partner.

People who thrive are so crystal-clear about their purpose and values that they have the confidence to **voice** their view, even when it's a **voice** of dissent or an unpopular opinion.*

*(Quick side note: I cover the topic of discovering your purpose and values in my book, 'Lead + Live: 6 Practices to Live Bigger.')

FIND YOUR VOICE 〉 VOICE YOUR VIEW 〉 BE UNDERSTOOD

Your **voice** is a powerful tool to be used respectfully and compassionately. So, I'm definitely not advising that you blast others with your divergent opinions. I'm recommending that you listen with the intent to truly hear what others have to say and that you calmly, clearly **voice** your authentic view.

All too often in life and business, people adopt opinions based on those around them. It's tough to be the only one in a meeting seeing an issue through a different lens. Just as it's hard to be the parent or spouse whose gut is saying to bring up something no one wants to discuss.

But burying your opinions and singing along with someone else's tune undermines your unique **voice** and your personal power. If you can't speak authentically, you're not being true to your purpose and values. This is not a path to thriving.

Finding and using your **voice** is a journey. It's entirely possible to have it at one point in your life and then lose it for a while.

This can happen when you go through difficult periods or when you're in a relationship or job that somehow tramples on your **voice**. It can also happen when you go through a major life change and need to reexamine who you are in the world.

*But fear not. Just as you can lose your **voice**, you can find it again. The key is giving yourself the time and space to redefine (or reconfirm) your purpose and values. Then you need to find the confidence to use your **voice** to live by them.*

Finding Your Voice

People who know themselves deeply and live their lives passionately tend to have something compelling to say. When they speak, people lean in a little.

I think this is because they're likely to just say what they mean, without adding extra content. They know what they believe and they say it, while others search for their own opinions as they speak.

I often see people struggle to find their voices. They may speak confidently in meetings or at a podium, but their voice is not their own. In some cases they've adopted a popular, safe view. In other cases, they're being a contrarian just to stand out.

It takes a certain amount of self-awareness and bravery to just say what you really think. And it takes a dose of humility to pipe down at the right times and learn from others.

I have 5 questions below for you to consider. Let these be indicators of how confident you are in your own voice.

1 Do you tend to soften your own opinions so they'll be more easily accepted?

2 Do you leave a conversation not feeling good about what you've said?

3 Do you feel people don't take your opinions seriously?

4 Are you often unsure of what your true opinion really is?

5 Do people seldom take action based on what you say?

If you answered 'yes' to any of these questions, you're still in the process of finding your voice. It's possible you place too much importance on what other people think of you, so you water down your true voice to avoid offending anyone. It's also possible you've been conditioned to defer to others.

Finding your voice starts with calming your mind, filtering other people's opinions, and listening intently for your own truth. Let yourself experiment with this. Over time it becomes a natural way of thinking.

Your Leadership Voice

Your voice is one of your most potent tools as a leader.

You can be visionary, brilliant and skilled, but if you can't convince others to support your mission, you won't survive as a leader. Simple as that.

I cringe when I hear people use their voices aggressively, but I know it's because they don't understand the arts of discourse and persuasion. They think power only comes in the form of intimidation. They're trying to strong-arm their way to success. It's certainly a path, but it's not one I recommend.

Instead I suggest you use your voice far more judiciously.

Here are 3 tips for advancing your persuasiveness:

1 **Everything starts with listening.** When you truly hear the other person's view, you can see where there are common goals. You can find middle ground. And you can overcome objections.

2 **Never raise your voice or use an irritated tone.** You've lost the race the moment this happens. If you find yourself growing irritated, take a breath. In fact take several. If you can't speak with calmness and compassion, reschedule the conversation.

3 **Notice what's in it for the other person.** How will they benefit from your plan coming to fruition? Or, how can you support them with something they want to bring to life?

Do You Inspire Action?

Being eloquent is lovely, but it's not essential to thriving.

The real issue is, do you speak in a way that inspires action? This is a mark that you're thriving as a leader and in life.

You may not have assessed the impact of your voice before. So consider it now.

After you've led a brainstorm discussion or a meeting ... what happens? If people leave the room with a clear mandate, motivated to bring ideas to life – that's leadership. If they arrive at the next meeting ready to discuss their progress and next steps – you're a rainmaker.

The same is true in your personal life. Do you leave conversations with loved ones feeling understood? If you've requested support or change, does it usually happen?

I've learned this in spades raising my son Adam, who's now a teen. I'm always conscious of my communication style with him, seeking to lead with empathy so he feels seen and heard.

If he's had a rough day at school, I'm careful to let him reveal his troubles on his own terms. I'll say things like, 'I can understand how angry you are about your test results. I suspect you're feeling frustrated.' Or, 'I can see you're managing a lot right now with school and swimming. It's ok to have moments of feeling overwhelmed.'

Steven Covey was a master of this in all aspects of his life. He said, "Seek first to understand, then to be understood."

Having a powerful voice has little to do with wit or presentation skills. It's about understanding people, and how to convey ideas in a way that creates understanding.

The only path to refining your voice is by increasing your awareness of those around you. Tune into how they feel when you speak. Notice if their energy drains when they speak to you or if they seem ready to take the world by storm.

Getting Past the Fear of Speaking Up

Let's start here: Are you overjoyed when you don't need to say anything in a meeting? Do you tend to clam up when things get tense at home?

Spontaneously voicing a clear, concise opinion can be intimidating. It's like the universe suddenly shines a spotlight on you and says, 'Go on, then. Sound smart.'

Some people live for these moments. It's ok if that's not you. But to thrive, you'll need to find a way to be at peace with speaking up.

Here are my top 5 tips for speaking up:

1 **Tune into your true opinion.** Don't let your mind be overrun with thoughts of what the 'correct' opinion is or what everyone else thinks. Listen to the information at hand and trust your own knowledge.

2 **Don't bother trying to impress people.** It's exhausting. Say what needs to be said in a straightforward way. There are no extra points for fancy words or phrasing. Brevity is the goal, but make sure you fully express your point.

3 **Notice your awesomeness.** Smarts come in many forms. Some people are brilliantly verbal. Don't let their form of brilliance devalue yours. Validate yourself constantly for your forms of brilliance.

4 **For work related matters, find your comfort zone.** If you're in accounting, say to yourself, 'What is my view on this from an accounting perspective?' If you're in HR, give an HR perspective. This will help you feel less exposed – you're not sharing a personal opinion, but a professional view.

5 **Form your thoughts.** Jot down notes as meetings are underway, recording your questions, concerns, ideas and opinions. Make them brief. When it's time to voice an opinion, quickly review them and identify the most salient points to say.

For tense personal conversations, it's ok to give yourself room to breathe. Rather than responding quickly in the moment, go away and think through or write down your thoughts. You'll be calmer and clearer. And less likely to say something you don't mean.

Voice

LEADING QUESTION

How often do I back down from saying what I really mean?

Wealth

Let's talk about **wealth**, which doesn't necessarily mean being rich beyond your wildest dreams.

WEALTH

Wealth is knowing you can cover the costs of what you need and reasonably want in life. I think of it as an emotional state rather than a number. It's about self-defined abundance.

Having **wealth** starts with knowing your unique financial priorities and making trade-offs that are aligned to those. Sometimes you may need to make tough choices, like holding off on a new car so you can pay down your mortgage, for example.

Financial dissatisfaction typically happens when you try to match an ideal of how you think you're supposed to live. This is also known as keeping up with the Joneses.

Contrary to what most people believe, having more and earning more aren't always tied to more contentment. They are if you don't have a roof over your head or you're wondering how you're going to put food on the table next week.

But if your basic needs are met, financial satisfaction is dependent on how you personally derive happiness and if you align your spending accordingly.

There are 3 components to financial satisfaction:

PERSONAL GROWTH

This is spending related to education and personal development for you and your children. It might include conferences, music lessons, retreats, art classes, saving for your MBA or your children's education.

⬆

LIFESTYLE: BEYOND THE BASICS

Everything from retirement savings to entertainment and travel. Your car, clothes, leisure activities, gym membership, art ... and whatever items and experiences make life abundant for you.

⬆

LIVING: YOUR MOST BASIC NEEDS

The cost of food, shelter and all of the fundamentals that make you safe and sound. This is the bottom rung of Maslow's Hierarchy of Needs.

Aim to break yourself of any tendencies to compare yourself to other people's versions of wealth. Focus your spending on your own priorities and interests.

Wealth starts with knowing what makes you thrive: your purpose in life and your values. Then, you align the way you earn and spend according to those priorities.

Some people are far happier working fewer hours at a lower salary so they have time to spend on other things – e.g., family, travel, volunteer work, education, artistic pursuits ... or countless other possibilities. Others love the thrill of a career that provides a hefty salary and tons of material perks.

If you decide to take a lower paying job that directly aligns to your passions, it will bring you more contentment than a vacation in Bali. Or, if you know that travel is your purpose in life, allocating more money on vacations will bring far more satisfaction than a sleek new car.

The key is knowing your personal definition of **wealth** and living by it. This unlocks a feeling of abundance, which is essential to mastering the art of thriving.

"Money is only a tool. It will take you wherever you wish, but it will not replace you as the driver."

Ayn Rand

Feeling Wealthy

For the most part, feeling wealthy is a matter of perspective. It's a mindset.

I've known multi-millionaires who feel a constant state of scarcity and worry about money. I've known people who earn an average salary and feel tremendous abundance.

But there are practical elements to feeling wealthy too. If you're ignoring your financial reality, you could be digging a deep hole for yourself and your family.

If you want to change your financial situation or simply feel better about your current circumstances, you need to take an honest look at where you are today.

Read these 7 statements. How many are true for you?

1 I meet my financial obligations easily every month.

2 I'm comfortable with my level of debt.

3 I'm comfortable with my level of retirement savings.

4 I have money set aside for a rainy day.

5 I have a reasonable amount of money to spend on the little extras in life.

6 I love the way I earn my living.

7 In general, I'm on top of my personal finances.

If one or more of these statements isn't true for you, this is an important reality check. Just one of these issues can completely negate your ability to feel safe and abundant.

Don't Fear Financial Success

I want to shatter a myth. Moving up the corporate ladder doesn't necessarily lead to a more stressful life. Making more doesn't have to be harder.

I've seen people hold themselves back from higher paying positions, assuming they'd have to sacrifice too much personally – thinking the weighty responsibility would be their undoing.

The fear is, 'If I'm this stressed out already, I don't even want to imagine the burden that comes a notch or more up the chain.'

Stop thinking you can't handle more responsibility because with the right tools, you probably can.

Consider this: the more senior your role, the more resources you have at your disposal. That means you'll likely have more people to support you and a larger budget to get things done.

If you're managing a high-salary job well, the work you're doing is more strategic. You're doing different tasks as someone in a less senior role, but you're not necessarily doing more work.

Personally, I noticed decreasing stress as I took on more responsible roles. I found that having more control over my destiny and more influence within the company made life noticeably easier. I could deliver bigger results faster because I could focus on the big picture. This gave me peace of mind.

If you're managing your vitality, voice and mindfulness, the odds are in your favor. You can take on more than you realize.

Your Wealth Priorities

Let's assume for the moment that your financial resources aren't infinite.

Don't spend all your energy wishing they were. This is a sure-fire energy drain and you may find yourself pining for more money your whole life. Get off this train now.

I want to teach you how to feel wealthy, which is substantially different than having unlimited funds.

You'll feel wealthy when the money you spend is allocated according to what you most love and value. Period.

Cautionary note: this doesn't mean you should spend untold sums on clothing, shoes and toys for your kids because you love them so enormously.

It means you need to look at what principles you value most in life and define your actions and spending according to those values.

Case in point: I have client who defines her most cherished values as 'Home & Hearth' and 'Love.' It makes perfect sense for her to focus her spending on creating a warm, nurturing living space and local pastimes that involved her husband and kids.

She travels far less than her friends and she doesn't spend a lot of money on dining or entertainment. But I can tell you with certainty she feels wealthy. Her spending is focused where it has the most benefit to her.

Another client sold a spectacular condo in Whistler to free up funds to travel abroad more. Since then, he's felt more of a sense of liberty. He makes the same money and he's spending the same money, but his life feels more decadent.

Make a commitment to yourself. Take some time this week to figure out your wealth priorities. Have your computer, iPad or journal handy. Jot down all the things you spend money on and the things you'd like to spend money on.

Use your gut. It will literally tell you your priorities. If you have an uneasy feeling about where your money is going right now, heed it. Change your ways now. Focus your spending more strategically. You'll notice an immediate sense of relief.

Shifting to Abundance

If abundance is a mindset, how do you acquire it?
It begins by noticing your beliefs about money and
any patterns of scarcity that you've adopted.

**People who feel abundant tend to
follow good money practices. Here are
6 practices to adopt in your own life
to create more ease with wealth:**

1 **Know how much money you want.** How much do you need
  to feel satisfied and abundant?

2 **Talk to your spouse or partner regularly about money.**
  Don't make it the dark, unpleasant topic no one wants to
  discuss. Bring it out into the light of day.

3 **Don't let your finances be vague.** Stay current with how much
  is in your bank accounts and investment accounts.

4 **Know how much you spend every month and on what.**
  Don't make it onerous, but have a method for knowing where your
  money is going.

5 **Pay down your credit card debt, if you have any.** If you can afford
  it, pay the full amount off every month. Debt weighs on your mind
  and drains your wealth.

6 **Find some joy in managing your money.** Approach conversations
  with the bank, your accountant, your investment advisor with a
  sense of optimism rather than dread. Really. Give it a go.

Wealth

LEADING QUESTION

What financial habit do I most need to change?

Happiness

You may be thinking, '**Happiness** is a practice?'
Indeed, it is. And not just a practice ... it's a choice.

HAPPINESS

VISION

WEALTH

MINDFULNESS

VOICE

VITALITY

Happiness isn't just for momentous occasions. It's something you create by living in alignment with who you really are.

The traditional idea about **happiness** is that if you do all the right things in life (go to the right school, choose the right job, marry the right person, etc.), you will have everything you want in life and then you'll be happy.

But thanks to a massive academic movement to better understand **happiness**, researchers have discovered otherwise.

What we now know is that happy people focus on just being who they are, deep down inside. They let their deepest desires guide all career and life choices. This leads to a life they love, and that's why they're happy.

But it's so easy to say, 'be who you are.' Most people assume they are already 'being who they are' ... after all, what other way is there to be?

The reality is you may be making unconscious choices to live according to someone else's ideals.

Maybe you let go of a passion for music to pursue a career in finance that seemed more prudent. Or you heeded your parents' advice to get a job right after college rather than traveling to Asia. Or you decided to forgo the MBA program you dreamed of for years to put a down payment on a house.

There are countless conscious and unconscious decisions over the course of your life that create the level of **happiness** you have today. If you've consistently made decisions that align to your true self and your values, you are far more likely to be happy than someone who has not.

To increase your **happiness** level, you need to bring more awareness to the choices you are making and be brave enough to go with your heart.

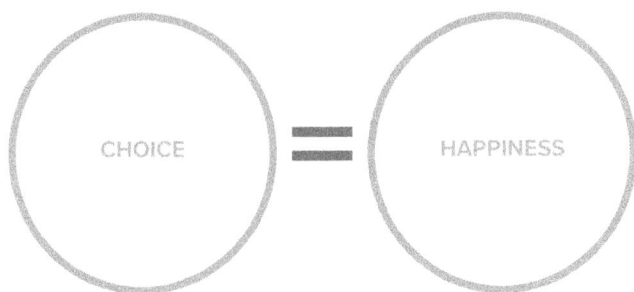

CHOICE = HAPPINESS

Happiness is important for obvious reasons. It's a nearly universal desire to live a fulfilled, content existence. This makes it a central element to thriving.

Happy people have more to offer the world. More energy for loved ones, creative endeavors, volunteering and community involvement. They are not addicted to the exhausting and addictive achievement cycle. Their enthusiasm for life comes from an ongoing sense of purpose and meaning, rather than short-lived bursts of accomplishment.

In the business world, **happiness** matters for more subtle reasons. Research shows happy people are more open-minded and more aware of everything around them. This allows them to be more innovative and resilient. These factors are tremendous advantages in the workplace, and every aspect of life.

Warning Signs of a Happiness Problem

I've observed something intriguing about happiness: A shocking number of people have no idea they're unhappy.

To a certain degree, this can be chalked up to denial. People don't understand how to become happier so they choose to not see the truth. I suspect they fear happiness is a fairy tale, and there's no sense seeking a fantasy.

But there is another big reason people refuse to see their happiness, or lack thereof. They aren't clear what reasonable metrics of happiness are. How happy should someone expect to be?

Here are 5 questions to help you determine if you've got a happiness problem.

1 Do you love your daily routine?

2 Do you know the bigger meaning of your life?

3 Do you have a true sense of connection to the people in your life?

4 Do you frequently experience joy?

5 If you could do your life over, would you do most major things the same way?

If you answered 'no' to any of these questions, you're in the majority. You have the right to experience more happiness in life.

This May Sound Harsh

Here's a fundamental truth: Big happiness requires a gigantic leap in self-responsibility.

Blaming other people for your problems and dissatisfaction will absolutely, unequivocally lead only to frustration and discontentment. Free yourself from this trap.

I'm about to say some things that may sound harsh.

Your parents are no longer to blame for the imperfections of your childhood. Your colleagues, managers and employees are not responsible for your lack-lustre luster moments at work. Your spouse or partner is not responsible for making you happy or helping you feel better about yourself.

If you're signing on the dotted line to believe any of these things, you're limiting your life and your joy.

I know how mind-bending this may be, particularly if you've walked some difficult roads in life. But the sooner you stop the blame-game, the sooner you can own your experience of life.

Focus instead on what you've learned from the roads you've traveled. You might be a compassionate and resilient person because of a difficult childhood. You might know a lot about your personal boundaries thanks to a challenging relationship. Maybe you're now a better manager thanks to the lessons from a spectacular failure at work.

Taking full responsibility for your life can feel scary at times. Just keep going. Don't let yourself believe any thoughts that tell you you're a victim or that other people have more influence on your life than you do.

Owning Your Life

Stop and consider this question for a moment:
Who's in charge of your life?

No really. I know the obvious answer is that you, of course, are fully in charge of your own life. But anyone who has a cap on their happiness level isn't always steering the ship.

Are any of these statements true for you?

1 I tend to make life choices based on what's smart or rational as opposed to what I truly want.

2 There are things in life I love to do, but almost never do anymore.

3 I'm not sure if what I do really matters in the grand scheme of things.

4 There are certain parts of my life I'm really dissatisfied with.

5 I blame my parents for the way some aspects of my life have played out.

If any of these are even partly true for you, consider it good news. It means you're starting to see ways to change so you can assume more control of your life.

Use these statements as clues to uncover when and why you let other people take charge. Ask yourself if it's worth it. Every time you turn an aspect of your life over to someone else, you lose the ability to choose what really makes you happy.

March to Your Own Drummer

You might be mystified when people say happiness comes from 'just being who you really are.'

After all, who else can you be?

The truth is, as a complex and intelligent being, you have the amazing capacity to morph into various versions of yourself. These are slightly (or dramatically) adjusted variations of 'the real you.'

You may have a version of you that makes your colleagues at work feel really comfortable around you. Another version may show up only around your closest friends. A different version still may be present when you're with your parents and extended family members.

It's entirely your choice to emphasize certain aspects of your personality in different situations. But this ability to morph can be taken too far. It can become a crutch that eventually prevents you from clearly seeing who you actually are.

If you're investing a lot of energy presenting 'appropriate' versions of yourself to different people, you're diluting your true personality and feelings.

You can't find happiness constantly accommodating other people. Examine how much time and energy you spend modifying your true nature. Then, ask yourself what it would take to start marching to the beat of your own drummer more often.

Happiness

LEADING QUESTION

Do I sacrifice my happiness for other people?

Vision

What will it take for you to thrive? It starts with **vision**.

It's personal. It's all about you. Your **vision** of thriving is the magical combination of circumstances that must exist for you to fully, enthusiastically love your life. It begins with wholeheartedly opening yourself up to vast possibilities.

Your **vision** will bring clarity, allowing you to see the route between where you are today and where you're going. It will require you to imagine and articulate how all of the pieces of your life can exist together in a beautiful, satisfying way.

*Your **vision** is yours alone to define, uniquely reflecting your innermost desires and dreams. Only you can bring it to the surface, but I aim to guide you in your search.*

Your vision must address all areas of your life, represented by these 3 major categories:

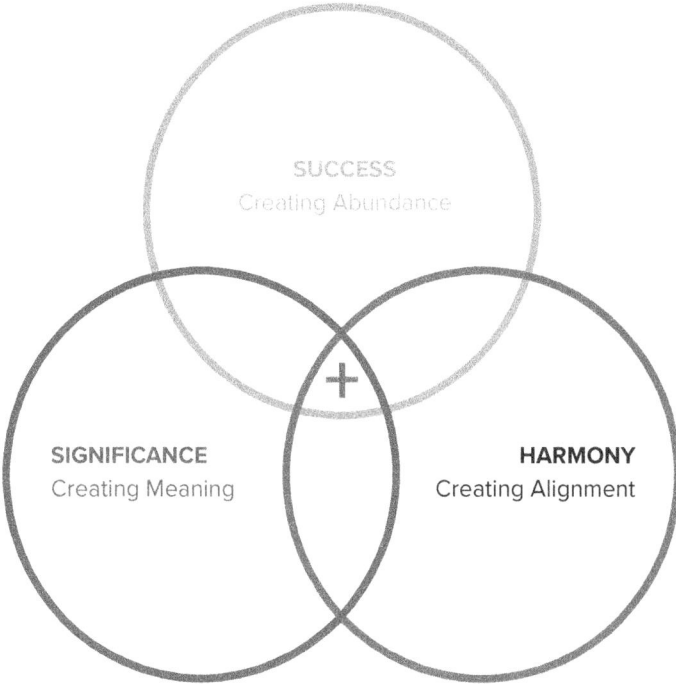

SUCCESS
Creating Abundance

SIGNIFICANCE
Creating Meaning

HARMONY
Creating Alignment

Success is about your material dreams. It includes near-term and long-term career aspirations. It also includes dreams for your home, possessions, wealth and resources.

SIGNIFICANCE: Creating meaning

Significance is about feeding your soul. This can be related to your love life, family, friendships, personal philosophies, religion, spirituality, hobbies, creative pursuits and volunteering.

HARMONY: Creating alignment

Harmony is when your actions are directly aligned to what matters most to you right now. It's about knowing your priorities and sticking to them.

The secret to thriving lies in placing equal priority on each part of this powerful trifecta. I've seen many people take a disproportionate approach to managing their lives, most often focusing on material success over significance and harmony. Thriving can never arise this way.

To create your **vision** of thriving, you will need to think big. Gigantic, actually. You'll need to envision possibilities far beyond your current circumstances.

You'll also need to ignore any complaints from your internal voice saying things like, 'That could never happen,' or 'That would be way too hard,' or 'It's crazy to dream this big.'

I want you to believe that whatever you envision can be your reality. After 15 years of coaching, I can confirm this isn't a platitude. Having a clear **vision** of thriving makes it possible to set your dreams in motion, taking the incremental steps needed to get you there.

Really … go ahead. Start dreaming crazy-big, and dwell in the possibility of your leadership and life.

Envision Success

The first thing to know about envisioning success is this: it's not as obvious as it may seem.

Your actual material needs and wants may be quite different from what you think. I had client who was nearly killing herself to support a decadent urban lifestyle that brought her very little happiness.

She kept assuming at some point she would hit an income level that would provide satisfaction. For years she pushed herself to earn more and have more.

When I asked her to really look at her true material desires, she realized she actually wanted to be in a smaller, quieter town where she could live on a vast acreage. She had been chasing and living a definition of success that simply didn't work for her.

I share her story to illustrate that when you envision success, you need to look internally. Don't defer to external ideas of success or old assumptions.

THE ENVISIONING PROCESS

Make sure you have at least an hour of quiet, uninterrupted time. Sit down with your iPad, computer or journal.

Here are 3 aspects of material success for you to brainstorm:

1 **Envision Your Home:** What type of physical environment is most suited to you? What would bring you satisfaction? Comfort?

2 **Envision Your Career:** How would you like to be earning your living 2 years from now? 5 years from now? What aspects of your career give you the greatest sense of fulfillment?

3 **Envision Your Lifestyle:** What resources and material possessions do you need to support the lifestyle you want? This can include anything from daycare support or a maid service, to a vacation home or new car.

Let your success vision be a crystal-clear, but evolving concept. Get as specific as you can now, and add color and texture to your vision over time as you learn more about yourself.

Envision Significance

Only you can know what gives your life meaning.

Significance is knowing who you are outside of your career, possessions and material success. If those things ceased to exist, what would your life be all about? Who are you beneath the material pursuits?

Your ultimate answer to this can be simple or multi-faceted, but it's crucial to explore the topic fully before you decide for sure. I urge you not to leap to a quick conclusion.

Kick-start your investigation here:

1 What current relationships make your life meaningful?

2 Are there any relationships you would like to create in the future to add meaning to your life?

3 What role (if any) does philosophy, religion or spirituality play in your life, or what role would you like it to play?

4 Do you have hobbies that add meaning to your life? If not, would you like to?

5 Do you have creative pursuits that add meaning to your life? If not, would you like to?

6 What role does volunteer work or community involvement play for you? Would doing more enrich your life's meaning?

After you've explored these questions and determined what gives your life meaning, ask yourself how much of your energy is devoted to these vital pursuits. To thrive, you will need to give these aspects of your life the time and focus they deserve.

A Harmonious Life

When you know your vision of material success and your sources for life's deeper meaning, you are ready for harmony, which is about letting these desires co-exist.

Harmony begins by not compartmentalizing your life. If you think of your life in terms of balancing categories (job, family, friends, health, community, etc.), you will inevitably drive yourself to frustration. Life has far too many categories to juggle simultaneously.

Instead, look at this current stage of your life and ask, 'What are my 3 to 5 biggest priorities right now?' Then, align all of your actions and decisions according to these priorities. This path leads to something much richer and more satisfying than 'balance.' It leads to harmony.

Let me explain this more concretely. Let's imagine a 37-year-old engineer named Alex whose vision for material success includes a contemporary 4-bedroom home in a suburb, 2 luxurious vacations a year and a certain sum of retirement savings by the time he's 55. Let's say he derives his significance in his children, life partner, artistic pursuits and competitive mountain biking.

Right now, Alex's kids are 3 and 5 years old. He's just made partner at his company and he's adjusting to this new level of responsibility. He decides that his top two priorities are his family and his job. He's chosen mountain biking as his third priority, because he wants to compete as much as he can while he's still relatively young.

He hasn't dropped his art, but he knows he will have much more time for this pursuit in 5 years or so when he's settled in his job. At an even later stage of life when his kids are older, it will move up much higher on his priority list.

What I'm saying is, life is not a one-act play. To thrive, you need to regularly reevaluate your priorities and invest your energy accordingly.

This doesn't mean you should give up certain pursuits you love until you're retired. It also doesn't mean you should be a one-trick pony and invest the majority of your energy in a single priority (like your career) at any stage of your life.

Harmony is about looking at the bigger picture and making choices that align all areas of your life.

Expand Your Sense of Possibility

There are a million directions you can take your life and career. Is anything stopping you from seeing your possibilities?

Having a vibrant sense of possibility changes everything. It puts your current situation into a bigger perspective, and a spark of enthusiasm in your heart. Possibility is why children are so full of hope and energy.

Too many adults let their sense of possibility erode. We're conditioned to think adults should be practical above all else.

So take a good, long look in the mirror. Are you limiting your life for the sake of practicality? If so, how will you feel about that at the end of the road?

Someone with a healthy sense of possibility has an inherent belief they can accomplish things in life. When new ideas or tasks arise out of the blue, they respond with a sense of curiosity and willingness. When a problem happens, they shift calmly to resolution-mode.

Being in a state of possibility makes it easier to move through life. It replaces feelings of dread, burden and complexity that often go hand-in-hand with adulthood.

So, what's your possibility level? Check out the following statements. Are any of these true for you?

1 I generally feel other people aren't as realistic as I am.

2 When I assess opportunities, I tend to see more 'cons' than 'pros.'

3 I don't see the point of taking a risk when there's a safe bet.

4 It's best to stick with my proven way of doing things.

5 I find that life has a way of slowly beating you down over time.

If any of these statements ring true for you, your possibility level needs a boost. It's time to shake up your way of thinking. You're in a rut or headed for one.

Make a concerted effort to look beyond current assumptions about your life and career. Turn those assumptions upside down ... imagine they don't limit you at all.

You will probably need to release some pessimism to get past your current beliefs about yourself and your possibilities.

Go ahead. Get out of your own way.

Vision

LEADING QUESTION

Do I have the guts to focus on 3 to 5 priorities for the time being?

Part Four:

ADVICE FOR YOUR JOURNEY

Thrive Thinking

All major artists – from Kandinsky and Warhol to Lady Gaga – have dared to express themselves uniquely. They've given themselves the freedom to be who they are, even when it seemed bizarre or incomprehensible to other people.

The same is true for anyone who masters the art of thriving. It takes a shift in thinking.

You need to believe you can concoct a vision of what your life can be and manifest it. To do this, you must believe you deserve to thrive. And that everyone around you – your family, friends, community and workplace – will be better off if you do.

Let me break it down.

Everything in life is a choice. I mean that literally. Just as you can choose to eat wholesome foods to create a healthier body, you can make choices that create every element of your life.

So, yes, you are what you eat. But more importantly, you are what you think.

Do you think you deserve to feel deeply satisfied with your life? If you don't, it won't matter how diligently you follow the 6 practices in this book. Thriving will escape you.

A thriving mentality requires:

1 **Desire:** Knowing how you want to feel every day and what a meaningful life is to you.

2 **Drive:** Concerted focus. A willingness to let go of things that aren't part of your life vision.

3 **Humility:** Your vision of thriving is no better or worse than someone else's. Live and let live.

4 **Patience:** Thriving is a lifelong endeavor. There will be hills and valleys. Get comfortable with uncertainty.

5 **Love:** Approach your life from a place of love. It's a basic human need. Make sure you're open to having it in your life in all its forms.

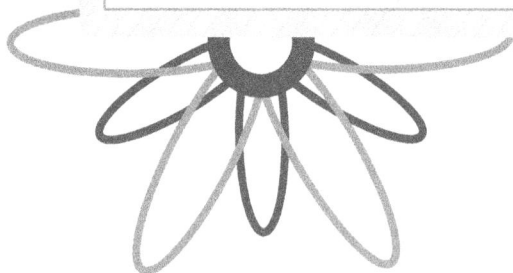

It's Your Life

Congratulations. You've gained the know-how to create a beautiful, abundant life for yourself and those you love.

But of course thriving doesn't happen simply by reading these chapters. It comes from consistently applying these practices in your everyday life.

I know you've heard tales of wildly accomplished individuals ending their days bitter, dissatisfied and searching for the meaning of life. Even so, you may find it overwhelming at times to take the steps needed to thrive.

So I want to tell you this: The greatest burden you can give those you love, is your own life unlived. Don't afflict them with your own unhappiness, boredom or regret.

Think of these words when the thriving practices feel hard. Think of the bigger picture of your life – how you want to feel about your choices at the end of the road. Do you want your loved ones to bear the weight of your discontent?

Choosing to thrive is a gift to everyone around you – family, friends, community and colleagues. It's not selfish to live your life well. Instead, it's a model for others to follow as they seek their own happiness.

Now that you know how to thrive, can you choose to live any other way?

Your beautiful life awaits.

Lisa

P.S. I love feedback. Please share your thoughts directly with me at:
lisa@lisamartininternational.com

Afterword

May I make a suggestion?

If you found this book of value, consider bringing the leadership development program, **LEAD + LIVE ADVANCED: 6 Practices to Master the Art of Thriving,** to your organization.

Just like this book, **LEAD + LIVE ADVANCED** offers the most current thinking in positive psychology and mindfulness to help leaders make major career and life goals a reality.

Program participants will harmonize their personal and professional lives to go beyond just living, to thriving.

LEAD + LIVE ADVANCED is a flexible, turnkey licensing solution that comes with all the tools required to cultivate high-impact, thriving leaders.

In other words, you get a proven program with all the training materials you need, including online self-assessments, facilitator guides, workbooks, PowerPoint Decks, posters and, of course, this book.

And you have the freedom to deliver **LEAD + LIVE ADVANCED** your way on your schedule.

Acknowledgments

My understanding of thriving comes not just from my personal experience, but many powerful influences in my life – most notably my husband, Rob, and son, Adam.

Adam continually reminds me what zest for life looks like – and really, isn't that one of the most magical things about being a parent? His curiosity, optimism and willingness to learn reinvigorate me whenever life feels hard.

Rob's unwavering ability to see life's big picture keeps me grounded. When I'm obsessing over details or experiencing worry, it's Rob who gently reminds of what's important and what's not. He's my North Star.

Other influences include people I've never met, but whose artistry inspires me to find beauty wherever I go. These include painters, sculptors, musicians and actors who are far too many to name. Art and music touch the soul, asking us all to experience life more fully.

And then we have the writers. Many authors have helped to shape my thinking on how to thrive. In particular, I'd like to acknowledge Shawn Achor, Martin Seligman, Marshall Goldsmith, Brené Brown and Cheryl Richardson.

Of course, I must say thank you to my clients. Every time I watch a client transform their life and begin to thrive, I'm struck with gratitude that I get to do this for a living. Thank you all for having the guts to live life on your own terms.

And, I honor all the dreamers who have dared to live wholeheartedly, including Audrey Hepburn, Jane Goodall, Andy Warhol and Herbert and Dorothy Vogel ... all of whom helped me see beauty in wildly different ways.

Lastly, thank you, reader. Here's to you for taking the time to reflect on what makes you thrive.

About the Author
Lisa Martin, PCC

Lisa Martin has made it her mission to help companies keep and cultivate leaders. She's the creator of the **Lead + Live Better**™ leadership programs; author of 5 books, including the bestselling **Briefcase Moms**; and a seasoned speaker, facilitator and executive coach.

For the past 15 years Lisa has designed and delivered leadership programs for PwC, TELUS, Vancouver Canucks, HSBC and UBC, to name a few.

Her powerful, easy-to-use **Lead + Live Better**™ turnkey leadership licensing solutions empower organizations to cultivate amazing leaders at every level.

She has coached thousands of people on the art of thriving as a leader and in life, and counseled companies on building leadership capacity.

As a speaker, Lisa is sought by international conferences, corporations and universities. She's known for her fun, straight-shooting speaking style and her intuitive sense for her audience.

She does all this as the founder of **Lisa Martin International**, a boutique leadership development firm with global scope, which equips organizations to deliver powerful leadership development in-house.

Lisa lives in North Vancouver with her husband, spirited teenaged son and two cats that act like toddlers.

You can find her at: **lisamartininternational.com**

"It's not selfish to live your life well."

Lisa Martin

Cornerview Press
Box 30075
North Vancouver, BC
Canada V7H 2Y8

Edited by Jacqueline Voci
Cover and text design by Melissa Hicks & Melanie Iu
Cover image by Getty Images
Author Photo by Linda Mackie

ISBN 978-0-9734560-4-2

Library of Congress information is available on request.

The examples I've used in this book reflect the stories I've been privileged to share in my work as a leadership coach. To respect my clients' privacy, I have changed their names and other identifying details.

lisaMARTIN
LEAD+LIVE BETTER

Lisa's **Lead+Live Better**™ programs deliver advanced leadership and life skills in a fun, intuitive and straight-shooting way.

LEAD

6 Skills to Be a
RockStar Leader

LEAD
advanced

6 Skills to Be the
Ultimate Executive

LEAD
for women

Briefcase Moms

LEAD+LIVE

6 Practices to
Live Bigger

LEAD+LIVE
advanced

6 Practices to Master
the Art of Thriving

lisamartininternational.com

www.ingramcontent.com/pod-product-compliance
Lightning Source LLC
Chambersburg PA
CBHW060323220326
41598CB00027B/4404